SUPERCARS

DRIVING THE DREAM

ADAM PHILLIPS

igloo

Published in 2010
by Igloo Books Limited
Cottage Farm
Sywell
NN6 0JB

www.igloo-books.com

ISBN 978-1-84852-959-5

10 9 8 7 6 5 4 3 2 1

Project management: Kandour Ltd
Editorial and design management: Emma Hayley and Jenny Ross
Author and project co-ordinator: Adam Phillips
Design and layout: Kurt Young
Cover pictures contributed by Evo magazine
Pictures contributed by Evo magazine, Ford Motor Company Ltd,
Bugatti Automobiles S.A.S, Aston Martin, Koenigsegg Automotive AB,
Mitsubishi Motors Ltd, Ariel Motor Company Ltd

Printed and manufactured in China

Contents

What makes someone want to buy a car that costs a small fortune? Or a very large one for that matter? Surely a nice little Japanese hatchback with a 1.4-litre engine will do the job. After all, you don't need 1,000bhp to pop down to the local shopping centre or to pick up the kids from school. But that's missing the point – us humans have a passion for pushing forward; for wanting to outdo and challenge ourselves, and supercars are one of the ultimate expressions of this desire. And people will always want to buy into that.

Naturally, there are those that merely want a supercar as a trophy; to be driven once in a while to impress their peers and to show the world that their bank balance is in fighting form. Equally, there are those who understand that only the best will do; who want to experience the sensation and thrill of cars designed for pure driver indulgence. And if we can't afford them, then we want to respect and admire the creativity and engineering that has made the supercar what it is today.

After all, the early days of supercar development were heady ones – bold but small steps into the future where one supercar would offer the greatest performance while the other would deliver the best driving experience. And now the

fruits of all that blood, sweat and tears over the past five decades are seemingly reaching their peak. From Britain and Italy through to America and Japan, the combined genius of designers and engineers has seen the supercars of today blend so many elements perfectly.

And they have to – we're a demanding bunch after all. We want those looks – the ones that linger in the mind well after glimpsing that exotic machinery for the first time. We want to know about the performance – the kind that defies belief when first scanning down a supercar's specifications. And we want the handling – the kind that offers huge grip, accessibility and feedback. Yes, we're a greedy bunch.

Modern supercars offer the best of all worlds (well, apart from the miles-per-gallon and luggage space that is) – and this book is a tribute to them. From supercars on a budget to exotica that can cost you a cool million, the automotive art featured in these pages show that we're all still as passionate about progress, and going fast, as we ever were.

The only question remaining is – if this is as good as it gets now, just what will be rolling down our roads in the future? We can't wait. Can you?

The History of the Supercar

There has never been a better time than now for supercar aficionados to indulge in their passion for automobile excellence. However, it has taken over 50 years of cumulative development and hard work by the world's greatest designers and engineers to bring us up to the modern day. Here we present some of the highlights of the supercar's emergence since its birth in the 1950s.

Mercedes 300SL Gullwing
(1954–1957)

This is not a true supercar, but it is one that showed the way forward because of its incredible technology and performance; the 3-litre engine, producing 240bhp, could make the sprint from 0-60 in 8.8secs and hit a top speed of 145mph.

Innovations in technology saw the 300SL become the first ever production car to have fuel injection, and the car featured a space-frame chassis which, because of the chassis running down either side of the car, meant the 300SL had to have those now-famous gullwing doors.

SPECIFICATIONS:

ENGINE	2996cc
MAX POWER	240bhp at 6,100rpm
MAX TORQUE	217lb ft at 4,800rpm
0-60MPH	8.8secs
TOP SPEED	135mph +

Ford GT40 MkIII
(1967)

Ford's race car version of the GT40 humiliated Ferrari at Le Mans in the latter half of the 1960s (see page 60). It also spawned a road-going version in 1967 that was panned by critics for its sloppy road manners. But real drivers didn't care about its manners, because the GT40 MkIII could see off its competitors in a straight line with the 306bhp produced by its 4.7-litre V8 engine – and boasted 0-60 in 5.5secs. Its top speed of 170mph also hinted at what the future held for true supercars. Only seven GT40s (MkIII) were ever built.

SPECIFICATIONS:

ENGINE	4736cc
MAX POWER	306bhp at 6,000rpm
MAX TORQUE	229lb ft at 4,200rpm
0-60MPH	5.5secs
TOP SPEED	170mph

Copyright Ford Motor Company Ltd

Lamborghini Muira
(1966–1972)

Unveiled in 1966, the Muira is what many believe to be the planet's first true supercar, partly because its mid-mounted engine was a world first. The greatest version of Muira is the SV produced at the beginning of the 1970s, which saw the original's 350bhp increased to 385bhp. The only

Lamborghini Muira SV specifications (1974-1982)

ENGINE	3929cc
MAX POWER	385bhp at 7,850rpm
MAX TORQUE	294lb ft at 5,750rpm
0-60MPH	6.0secs
TOP SPEED	180mph

problem with the Muira is that the front end is prone to lift at high speeds.

Other key cars from the 1960s: Jaguar E-Type, Ferrari 365 GTB Daytona, Corvette Sting Ray, De Tomaso Mangus

Lamborghini Countach 25th Anniversary (1989–1990)

Lamborghini Countach
(1974–1990)

It's one of the defining shapes in car history – the prototype Countach, which was shown for the first time in 1971, was greeted with rapture by the crowds. The replacement for the Muira, the sleek, sensual lines had been supplanted with dramatic lines and a wedge shape that would come to dominate the supercar world for the next ten years. The first Lamborghini Countach to be released (the LP400) featured a 3.9-litre V12 engine that could make the sprint from 0-60 in 5.6secs. Several incarnations of the Countach, which included the celebrated 5-litre Countach QV in 1985, followed over its illustrious 17-year reign as the king of the supercars. It has to be said though that the Countach represents the ultimate old-school supercar – it offered a driving experience that had to be learned; simply getting behind the wheel and flooring it was not to be recommended.

LP400 specifications (1974-1982)	
ENGINE	3929cc
MAX POWER	375bhp at 8,000rpm
MAX TORQUE	268lbft at 5,000rpm
0-60MPH	5.6secs
TOP SPEED	180mph +

BMW M1
(1978–1981)

The M1 is one of the unsung heroes of the 1970s. It was BMW's first (and, so far, only) foray into creating a mid-engined supercar, and it could have worked out if the project hadn't been besieged by problems. It was intended that the M1 would be styled and built by Lamborghini, but because the raging bull was experiencing money woes, Bauer, in Germany, produced the car for BMW. The car had been intended for the track but these plans fell through. It's a tragedy because the road-going M1 put the wind up its Italian rivals by offering the same levels of grip but pairing it with forgiving handling and bullet-proof reliability.

Specifications

ENGINE	3453cc
MAX POWER	277bhp at 6,500rpm
MAX TORQUE	243lb ft at 5,000rpm
0-60MPH	5.6secs
TOP SPEED	162mph

Other key cars from the 1970s: Maserati Bora, Porsche 911 2.7 RS, Porsche 911 Turbo, Aston Martin V8 Vantage.

Lotus Turbo Esprit
(1980–1992)

Lotus Turbo Esprit SE (1989)

The Lotus Esprit has had a long and illustrious history dating back to when the car was first introduced in 1976. One of the most revered versions was the Turbo that first surfaced in 1980 and featured a four-cylinder aluminium engine that could produce 210bhp. The Esprit's 'credentials' were further increased thanks to a movie appearance – the Turbo was James Bond's vehicle of choice (both on the road and underwater) in The Spy Who Loved Me. Over the decades there have been numerous incarnations of the Esprit, but its production run (that spanned an incredible 28 years) came to a close on February 21st, 2004.

Specifications

ENGINE	2174cc
MAX POWER	210bhp at 6,250rpm
MAX TORQUE	200lb ft at 4,500rpm
0-60MPH	5.6secs
TOP SPEED	150mph

Ferrari 288 GTO
(1984–1985)

The mid-engined GTO is actually the forefather of the classic F40, but this 1980s supercar has earned its rightful place in the history books because its body was manufactured from composite materials such as carbon fibre – making it one of the very few cars to feature such race-developed technology. These lightweight materials coupled with a twin-turbo 2.8-litre V8 engine meant that the GTO was an extremely quick car with handling that was, let's just say, best exploited by the 'experienced driver'.

Ferrari 288 GTO specifications

ENGINE	2855cc
MAX POWER	400bhp at 7,000rpm
MAX TORQUE	365lb ft at 3,800rpm
0-60MPH	4.7secs
TOP SPEED	188mph

Ferrari Testarossa specifications

ENGINE	4942cc
MAX POWER	390bhp at 6,300rpm
MAX TORQUE	354lb ft at 4,500rpm
0-60MPH	5.3secs
TOP SPEED	180mph

Ferrari Testarossa
(1984–1992)

Aimed at being more of a GT than a hardcore road racer, the Testarossa ('Red Head') showed Ferrari heading in a more refined direction while retaining the astonishing speed and acceleration that all supercar owners demand. And the flat-12 engine saw to that with its 390bhp.

Other key cars from the 1980s:
Aston Martin Bulldog,
Aston Martin Vantage Zagato,
Ruf CTR Yellowbird.

Porsche 959
(1987–1991)

Trust Porsche to come up with the 959, able to hit 0-60 in under 4secs. This phenomenal acceleration was achieved using a rear-mounted twin-turbo flat-six engine that produced 450bhp. To get such power down onto the road, the 959 featured four-wheel drive paired with a six-speed gearbox, and the kind of stability needed to hit a cool 197mph.

Porsche 959 specifications

ENGINE	2850cc
MAX POWER	450bhp at 6,500rpm
MAX TORQUE	369lb ft at 5,000rpm
0-60MPH	3.6secs
TOP SPEED	197mph

Ferrari F40
(1987–1992)

Released to celebrate the company's 40th anniversary, the F40 was the last road car that the marque's creator, Enzo Ferrari, commissioned before he passed away – but what a swansong. It looked more like a racing car than a supercar and it featured a 2.9-litre V8 engine that would see a brave driver propelled to over 200mph. The car is, of course, not for the faint-hearted but its position as one of the iconic supercars of any age is indisputable.

Ferrari F40 specifications

ENGINE	2936cc
MAX POWER	478bhp at 7,000rpm
MAX TORQUE	425lb ft at 4,000rpm
0-60MPH	3.9secs
TOP SPEED	201mph

Bugatti EB110
(1992–1995)

It was supposed to be the rebirth of the Bugatti brand and, at first, the future was looking bright for the marque. While the EB110's looks may have been controversial, the Bugatti was a true supercar with staggering performance; it featured, thanks to the chassis and four-wheel drive, a colossal amount of grip to make the most out of all that power. Two versions were available – the 'humble' GT with 553bhp and the Supersport which boasted 603bhp. But alas, the Bugatti dream imploded in 1995 when the company went bust, mainly because of the global recession.

Ferrari Testarossa specifications	
ENGINE	3500cc
MAX POWER	603bhp at 8,250rpm
MAX TORQUE	479lb ft at 4,250rpm
0-60MPH	3.1secs
TOP SPEED	218mph

Jaguar XJ220
(1992–1994)

Ferrari Testarossa specifications	
ENGINE	2498cc
MAX POWER	542bhp at 6,500rpm
MAX TORQUE	472lb ft at 5,000rpm
0-60MPH	3.6secs
TOP SPEED	210mph +

Quite frankly, the Jaguar supercar was something of a debacle. Back in 1988 customers were bedazzled by promises of a huge V12 engine, coupled with a four-wheel drive, when the XJ220 prototype was unveiled. Down went the deposits as (very rich) people waited for the car's arrival in 1992. The trouble was that Jaguar replaced the engine with a V6 and dumped the four-wheel drive. Some angry customers withdrew their orders and demanded their deposits back; legal wranglings ensued. Add to this a world recession, and Jaguar's supercar foundered. The sad fact is that on its release, the XJ220 was still a fantastically fast car boasting supreme handling (in the dry) – and then there were those striking looks.

McLaren F1
(1993–1997)

Ferrari Testarossa specifications	
ENGINE	6064cc
MAX POWER	627bhp at 7,400rpm
MAX TORQUE	479lb ft at 4,000rpm
0-60MPH	3.2secs
TOP SPEED	240mph

Until recently, the McLaren F1 was the fastest car on the planet. Its BMW 6.1-litre V12 engine produced a staggering 627bhp and could propel the car up to 240mph. And never mind the 0–60 time – the F1 could hit 100mph in just 6.3secs. The key to the McLaren's success was the fact it was created entirely from carbon fibre and built on a philosophy that demanded it be put together with absolute precision. The resulting car can seat three people – the driver in the middle with two passengers to the side and back of him. The McLaren's production came to an end when customers decided that the price tag of £635,000/US$1,000,000 was perhaps stretching even them a little too much. The McLaren would also carve out a name for itself on the track by winning the Le Mans 24-hour race in 1995.

Ferrari F50
(1995–1997)

What happens when you put a Formula One engine into a production car? Well, trust Ferrari to be the ones bold enough to try it – and, of course, to get it right with the F50. The 4.7-litre V12 lump featured in the supercar was a direct descendant of the engine that nearly earned Alain Prost top honours in the 1990 F1 World Championship. Just as important to the F50's achievement as a true race car made for the road was its easy-to-access driving experience – the F50 left its forefather the F40 for dead on a twisty track, so sweet and accessible was its handling.

Ferrari Testarossa specifications	
ENGINE	4698cc
MAX POWER	513bhp at 8,000rpm
MAX TORQUE	347lb ft at 6,500rpm
0-60MPH	3.7secs
TOP SPEED	202mph

The Modern Supercar

Here is the culmination of what the best minds in the supercar business have to offer thanks to the last 50 years. From GTs through to roadsters, all the supercars featured here offer the true car-lover a wealth of treasures to indulge themselves in; looks that are intoxicating; performance that is G-force defying; and a driving experience that is truly unforgettable. Welcome to the state-of-the-supercar-art...

Aston Martin Vanquish S

The arrival of the original Vanquish and this, its more powerful brother the Vanquish S, has ushered in a new era for Britain's most iconic sports car company…

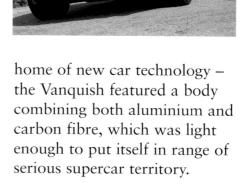

When Aston Martin unveiled the Vanquish in 2001, first impressions had to count – the Ford-owned company was coming out of the recession-ridden 1990s and needed an all-new flagship car to show the world that they were more than their classic DB7 coupe. Thanks to Ford's vision for the company and car designer maestro Ian Callum, jaws dropped to the floor when the car was first shown – the Vanquish was that striking; that poised; that menacing; that… British.

Featuring a V12 6-litre engine pumping out 460bhp, those bold good looks were backed up with an equally impressive driving experience. Ford wanted Aston Martin to become the home of new car technology – the Vanquish featured a body combining both aluminium and carbon fibre, which was light enough to put itself in range of serious supercar territory.

But the car marque's crowning glory is the Vanquish S. Debuted at the Paris Motor Show, France, in 2004, the S is the fastest production model Aston Martin has ever made. The 48-valve V12 6-litre engine now produces 520bhp over the previous Vanquish's 460bhp, and it can top 200mph. The S also features stiffer springs and dampers, plus shorter steering arms to give drivers the ultimate handling package.

24

"The Vanquish S is the fastest production model Aston Martin has ever made"

From Start To Finish

It takes 396 hours for Aston Martin's engineers at the Newport Pagnall factory, in the UK, to hand-build the Vanquish S; the interior alone takes more than 70 hours to craft, and features eight hides of leather.

Nip And Tuck

Cosmetically the S has been given subtle tweaks over the original Vanquish; as well as changes to the car's nose, it has also a raised lip on the boot to aid stability and balance while reducing lift.

What Lies Beneath

The Vanquish was always intended to show off Aston Martin as a hotbed of cutting edge technology. This is perfectly reflected by the materials that make up the car – aluminium is used for the bulkheads and floor while the windshield pillars and centre tunnel are made from carbon fibre.

Something Old, Something New

Designed by car industry legend Ian Callum, the Vanquish manages to blend perfectly the old and the new into a modern and fresh look. Callum is reported to have said that it was the DB4 GT Zagato from the 1960s that fuelled his vision for the Vanquish.

Copyright Aston Martin

Aston Martin Vanquish S: The Specifications

ENGINE	Fuel injected 48-valve V12		variable power assist	SUSPENSION REAR	Double wishbones with
VALVETRAIN	DOHC 4 valves / cyl	BRAKES FRONT	Ventilated & grooved		monutube dampers, coil
DISPLACEMENT	5935cc		with six callipers/		springs & anti-roll bar
MAXIMUM POWER	520bhp at 7,000rpm		378mm/15in	KERB WEIGHT	1875kg/4134lbs
MAXIMUM TORQUE	425lb ft at 5,800rpm		370mm/14.5in	LENGTH	4665mm/184in
TRANSMISSION	Six-speed manual with	BRAKES REAR	Ventilated & grooved	WIDTH	1923mm/76in
	paddle shifting		with four callipers/	HEIGHT	1318mm/52in
0–60MPH	4.7secs		330mm/13in	WHEELS FRONT	9 x 19in
0–125MPH	9.8secs	SUSPENSION FRONT	Double wishbones with	WHEEL REAR	10 x 19in
MAXIMUM SPEED	200mph +		monutube dampers, coil		
STEERING	Rack and pinion with		springs & anti-roll bar		

Aston Martin DB9

While the Vanquish showed the world where Aston Martin's future lay, it's the DB9 that has further secured their place as one of the most desirable brands on the planet...

The DB7 was an iconic British car. The problem was that the DB7 had been around for a while and was beginning to show its age. It needed an all-new replacement – something that would put the wind up Ferrari and Porsche; while the Vanquish demonstrated that Aston had its eye firmly on the future, they still needed a lower priced car that would help the company shift 5,000 cars a year. The DB9 is that car – built at Aston Martin's all-new factory in Gaydon, UK, it is regarded as one of the greatest GTs ever built.

Its low, sleek and muscular looks can be credited to design maestro Ian Callum who handed over the baton to Henrik Fisker to complete what many argue is the most beautiful car on sale today. But the DB9's beauty isn't merely skin deep – under the exterior is a wholly new platform. Named the VH (Vertical and Horizontal), it's constructed from aluminium, and all the major mechanical and body components have been engineered from aluminium, magnesium or lightweight composite materials. This means that with its V12 450bhp engine, the DB9 is able to propel itself at a fierce pace on the straights because of its relative lightness but also to corner confidently because of its rigidity. Most importantly, the driver never feels left out, or scared, by the DB9. This accessibility is easily managed by either a manual six-speed gearbox or a six-speed ZF automatic with paddle shifts that, while shaving 0.2secs off the car's 0–60 time, is highly regarded for its suppleness and smoothness.

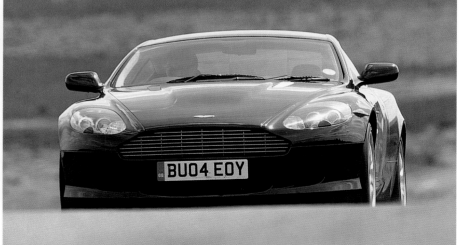

29

DB9 V12

Punishing The Prototypes

53 DB9 prototypes were made and put through their paces to ensure that the cars could cut it in extreme climates – from the gruelling conditions of Death Valley and the Arctic Circle through to its mechanics being stretched on the Nürburgring in Germany.

Delight In The Details

The DB9's cockpit has a wealth of quality touches – the glass starter button in the centre console shimmers red when the ignition is switched on, and once the engine is turned on the button lights up blue.

Personalised For Perfection

There are 29 colours available but Aston Martin will let you choose any you want at an extra cost. As well as a multitude of different leather options, four different woods are also available for the Aston's interior – mahogany, walnut, bamboo and piano black.

Taking A Different Tach

The rev counter featured in the DB9 actually runs anti-clockwise which echoes early Aston Martins such as the Atom and DB2. You won't find a red line on the tachometer either – instead a red light appears once the maximum revs are hit.

Swan Song

The DB9's doors don't open like the average coupe's – they actually pull upwards at a 12? angle to help the driver gain easier access to the cabin.

Copyright Aston Martin

Aston Martin DB9: The Specifications

ENGINE	Fuel injected 48-valve V12	STEERING	Rack and pinion with Servotronic speed-sensitive power-assist	SUSPENSION REAR	Double wishbones with monutube dampers, coil springs & anti-roll bar
VALVETRAIN	DOHC 4 valves / cyl				
DISPLACEMENT	5935cc				
MAXIMUM POWER	450bhp at 6,000rpm	BRAKES FRONT	Ventilated & grooved with six callipers/ 355mm/14in	KERB WEIGHT	1710kg/3770lbs (manual) 1800kg/3968lbs (auto)
MAXIMUM TORQUE	420lb ft at 5,000rpm				
TRANSMISSION	Six-speed manual or six-speed auto	BRAKES REAR	Ventilated & grooved with four callipers/ 330mm/13in	LENGTH	4710mm/185in
				WIDTH	1875mm/74in
0–60MPH	4.7secs (manual) 4.9secs (auto)			HEIGHT	1270mm/50in
		SUSPENSION FRONT	Double wishbones with monutube dampers, coil springs & anti-roll bar	WHEELS FRONT	8.5 x19in
0–125MPH	4.9secs (manual) 5.1secs (auto)			WHEEL REAR	9.5 x 19in
MAXIMUM SPEED	186mph				

Aston Martin DBR9

Aston Martin has wanted to return to the international motor racing scene for decades and this is how they are doing it – with the DBR9. Based on the DB9 and featuring the same aluminium chassis, the racing car has had some major modifications to make sure it's up to the job of winning major competitions.

The DBR9's engine produces 600bhp compared to the DB9's 450bhp while the suspension set-up boasts up-rated components plus a revised geometry. The car now features carbon brakes and a six-speed sequential gearbox mounted on the rear axle. The DBR9's aerodynamics have been optimised to produce the best possible performance on the track and the panels of the racer are also handmade from carbon fibre composite to ensure the car meets competition weight regulations.

The DBR9 has already experienced major success on its debut at the 53rd Annual 12 Hours of Sebring, Florida in March where Aston's team gleaned itself a GT1 class victory.

Aston Martin V8 Vantage

This is what everyone is calling the new 'baby' Aston, but it's destined to make one very big splash when it finally touches down...

It could be argued that the V8 Vantage is the single most important Aston ever to be built. It's the most affordable Aston to be made available to the masses with a price of £74,500 (US price upon application), which will put it in line with the likes of the Porsche 911.

That's virgin territory for Aston Martin, but they are all set to hit the mark. Using their unique aluminium VH platform, as used by the DB9 but shortened with stiffer suspension, the V8 Vantage has a howling 4.3-litre engine providing the firepower. While the V8 Vantage 'only' features a V8, it can match the V12-driven DB9 because it's lighter – giving it a 0–60 time of 4.8secs and

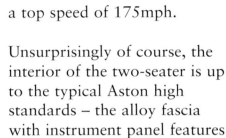

a top speed of 175mph.

Unsurprisingly of course, the interior of the two-seater is up to the typical Aston high standards – the alloy fascia with instrument panel features beautifully finished aluminium. But optional mahogany, walnut or bamboo can be included.

As for the build quality, 78 prototypes have been clocking up 1,500,000 miles between them. The Nürburgring, Germany, and the Nardo test track, Italy, have been used to develop and hone the V8 Vantage's handling. In fact, one V8 Vantage was challenged with the task of racking up 5,000 miles round the Nürburgring, which it did without breaking its stride.

"*The Aston Martin V8 Vantage is exotica defined, and put up against its competitors you have to ask yourself – which one is the more desirable?*

Which one has that 'X factor' which elevates it beyond mere sports car?

The answer is staring you in the face…"

Wait-y Issues...

To make sure the V8 Vantage keeps that important air of exclusivity, production of the car will be capped at 2,500 per year. Expect epic waiting lists – for the driver slapping down his deposit today, you can expect to wait until 2007 before it appears on the driveway.

Designer Departed

The good-looking V8 Vantage was designed by Henrik Fisker (who also designed the DB9). He has since departed Aston Martin and moved to California to set up an automotive design and customization company.

Weight A Minute...

The front-engined V8 Vantage has the spot-on weight distribution and offers the ideal set-up for any self-respecting sports car. The Aston's dry-sump lubrication system means that the engine can be placed lower in the body, meaning a lower centre of gravity. The result – better balance and stability.

Aston Martin V8 Vantage: The Specifications

ENGINE	All alloy quad overhead camshaft 32 valve V8		
VALVETRAIN	DOHC 4 valves / cyl		
DISPLACEMENT	4280cc		
MAXIMUM POWER	380bhp at 7,000rpm		
MAXIMUM TORQUE	302lb ft at 5,000rpm		
TRANSMISSION	Six-speed manual		
0–60MPH	4.8secs		
MAXIMUM SPEED	175mph		
STEERING	Rack and pinion with power assist		
BRAKES FRONT	Ventilated & grooved steel discs with four-piston monobloc callipers/ 355mm/14in, ABS		
BRAKES REAR	Ventilated & grooved steel discs with four-piston monobloc callipers/ 330mm/13in, ABS		
SUSPENSION FRONT	Independent double aluminium wishbones with coil over aluminium monutube dampers & anti-roll bar		
SUSPENSION REAR	Independent double aluminium wishbones with coil over aluminium monutube dampers & anti-roll bar		
KERB WEIGHT	1570kg/3461lbs		
LENGTH	4383mm/173in		
WIDTH	1866mm/73in		
HEIGHT	1255mm/49in		
WHEELS FRONT	8.5 x 18in		
WHEEL REAR	9.5 x 18in		

B Engineering Edonis

When Bugatti crashed and burned in the 1990s, a small group of ex-employees decided to take their destiny into their own hands and produce a supercar...

The Edonis is unusual. Not just in the way it looks with its bizarre lines and curves. The company behind this supercar, isn't interested in becoming a major player. All B Engineering ever wanted the supercar to be was a showcase for cutting edge technology that represented the excellence of both the company and the region where it is built – Modena, Italy, home of the supercar.

The number of staff may be small but many have worked for some of the greatest supercar makers of all time – Ferrari, Lamborghini and Maserati, to name but a few. In fact, the owner of the company, Jean-Marc Borel, used to be the vice chairman of Bugatti.

B Engineering's links with Bugatti form the core of the Edonis–when Bugatti declared bankruptcy in 1995, 21 leftover carbon fibre tubs from the Bugatti EB110 were acquired by B Engineering to create the Edonis. At the heart of the car's hand-built aluminium body is an extreme engine, an evolution of the EB110's – a 3.7-litre V12 with twin turbochargers, plus a six-speed manual gearbox.

With project director, Nicola Materazzi, who is famous for the classic handling of the Ferrari, it's perhaps predictable that the Edonis should become renowned for its precision steering and abundant feel.

"The Edonis is B Engineering's first and last car. All the company ever wanted the car to be was a showcase for cutting edge technology"

Record Breaker
A 720bhp version of the Edonis managed to break the circuit record of the Nardo race circuit in Italy by lapping at 223mph.

Named And Famed
The word Edonis is actually the Greek word for pleasure. And only a select few will be privileged enough to experience the car – just 21 will be made. B Engineering decided to make 21 because the Edonis is the first car of the 21st century.

Keeping It In The Family
B Engineering has stayed true to its vision of creating a supercar that uses all the incredible resources of the Modena area – local body builders, casters, upholsterers, pattern makers and others were called in to produce the Edonis.

Perfect Supercar CV
The Edonis's project director, Nicola Materazzi, has a resumé that screams supercar pioneer – he was the main contractor for the likes of Bugatti, and then from 1980, he worked for Ferrari on projects such as the GTO Evoluzione and F40. He was also top dog at Ferrari's F1 research and design division.

gineering Edonis (720bhp version): The Specifications

E	Twin turbocharged V12	MAXIMUM SPEED	223mph	SUSPENSION REAR	Double wishbon
RAIN	DOHC, 5 valves / cyl	STEERING	Rack and pinion with		coil springs, gas
CEMENT	3760cc		power assist		& anti-roll bar
UM POWER	720bhp at 8,000rpm	BRAKES FRONT	Cross-drilled & ventilated	KERB WEIGHT	1500kg/3307lbs
UM TORQUE	590lb ft at 5,250rpm		discs, ABS/335mm/13in	LENGTH	4350mm/171in
MISSION	Six-speed manual	BRAKES REAR	Cross-drilled & ventilated	WIDTH	1998mm/79in
PH	4secs		discs, ABS/335mm/13in	HEIGHT	1120mm/44in
		SUSPENSION FRONT	Double wishbones with		
MPH	8.2secs		coil springs, gas dampers		
			& anti-roll bar		

Ferrari Enzo

Is it beauty or the beast? It doesn't really matter, the Enzo defines what the supercar moniker is all about...

Explosive, aggressive, uncompromising. Named after the company's founder Enzo Ferrari, who died in 1988, the Enzo is the marque's fastest ever road-going car with a top speed of over 217mph, and the looks penned by Pininfarina are pure Formula One drama. That F1 nose, the angular body and those venturis shout to even the most casual of observers that this car is the closest a driver will ever get to feeling like Michael Schumacher.

With 660bhp produced by an ultra lightweight aluminium 6-litre V12 engine, the Enzo can devour many of its modern day competitors with a 0–60 time of 3.5secs.

Ferrari have made sure that the Enzo makes the most of its gigantic power by using its hi-tech ASR traction control system and an F1-style six-speed paddle shift that can snap through the gears in milliseconds. The Enzo's handling is legendary as

well – its chassis is constructed from carbon fibre and Kevlar honeycomb, which provides the Enzo with its extreme rigidity and strength; while that F1 nose, with its three air intakes, helps to keep the car glued to the road as it increases in speed, while keeping the V12 cool. Stopping capability is vital for such explosive thrust – and the carbon ceramic brakes with ABS are more than a match for such a punishing job.

Open the Enzo's scissor doors and there's easy access to the carbon fibre and leather cabin. The steering wheel has a multitude of F1-style buttons mounted on it for controlling everything from race settings to turning off the ASR. And for that extra Grand Prix touch, there are LEDs running along the top of the wheel, which act as a rev counter.

"The Enzo is Ferrari's fastest ever road-going car with a top speed of over 217mph"

Going, Going, Gone

Like any respectable supercar, limiting the numbers that can be bought is paramount. Initially, only 349 Enzos were made to order, and Ferrari sold every single one of them before they'd even shown a single picture or spec list of the car. The final figure for the number of Enzos assembled is 400 – one more than planned, with the extra car being auctioned off to raise money for the 2004 Asian tsunami appeal.

F1 Champ Elevates Enzo

Formula One champion Michael Schumacher had a firm hand in developing the Enzo. He drove several prototypes of the supercar and gave his thoughts on all aspects of the Enzo, from its performance to the driving position. In fact, thanks to Schumacher, there are 16 different pedal settings available to choose from.

Sky's The Limit

It would appear that the Enzo's value doesn't depreciate. If you want proof–in 2004, the Enzo became eBay Motors' most expensive car ever sold when a Swiss man (bidding from Brazil) made a winning bid of £544,000/US$1,038,227 – a brand new Enzo is worth £450,000/US$670,000.

Pulling Power

A survey by the RAC Foundation, based in Britain, discovered that 86 percent of British men would rather spend the weekend with a Ferrari Enzo than hang out with former Baywatch star Pamela Anderson.

Ferrari Enzo: The Specifications

ENGINE	Aluminium V12	**STEERING**	Rack & Pinion with power assist	**SUSPENSION REAR**	Double wishbones with pushrod links, coil springs, gas dampers & anti-rollbar
VALVETRAIN	DOHC, 4 valves / cyl with Continuously Variable Timing	**BRAKES FRONT**	Ventilated carbon-ceramic discs with 6-pot callipers, ABS/380mm/15mm		
DISPLACEMENT	5988cc			**KERB WEIGHT**	1365kg/3009lbs
MAXIMUM POWER	660bhp at 7,800rpm	**BRAKES REAR**	Ventilated carbon-ceramic discs with 4-pot callipers, ABS/380mm/15in	**LENGTH**	4702mm/185in
MAXIMUM TORQUE	485lb ft at 5,500rpm			**WIDTH**	2035mm/80in
TRANSMISSION	Six-speed sequential			**HEIGHT**	1147mm/45in
0–60MPH	3.5secs	**SUSPENSION FRONT**	Double wishbones with pushrod links, coil springs, gas dampers & anti-roll bar	**WHEELS FRONT**	9 x 19in
0–125MPH	6.5secs			**WHEELS REAR**	12 x 19in
MAXIMUM SPEED	217mph +				

Ferrari F430

The Lamborghini Gallardo, the Ford GT and the Aston Martin V8 Vantage... yes, Ferrari may have been facing increased competition over the past couple of years but trust them to come out fighting...

The F430 had a tough act to follow – Ferrari's illustrious reputation for creating exceptional sports coupés is unrivalled. Designed by Pininfarina, the 360 Modena replacement is a masterclass in mixing the sensual with the angular, and blending such seemingly diametric elements into a alluring body shape.

The successor to the acclaimed 360, the F430 is constructed entirely from aluminium and features a brand new 4.3-litre V8 engine that boasts far more torque than its forebearer and produces 483bhp – the car has a 0–62 time of 4secs and a top speed of 195mph. The F430 features a six-speed manual as standard and, as an option, a F1 paddleshift that can now move through those gears quicker than the previous incarnation found in the 360.

The F430 also has some new Formula One-sourced tricks up its sleeve for the driver to indulge in. The 'manettino' – which is a switch that can be flicked between various different modes – Ice, Wet, Sport, Race and CST – and lets you, with a simple flick, automatically alter the F430's settings such as dampers, traction control plus the speed of the F1 gearshifts.

The F430 also features an electronic differential. This e-diff aids torque distribution to the rear wheels, so if over-keen driving sees the back end starting to slide out, the clutches inside the e-diff quickly send torque to the wheel that has the most traction. Thanks to this unique e-diff, the F430 has been acclaimed for its benign handling and the ability to conquer corners with absolute and utter controllable ease.

"The F430 is acclaimed for its benign handling and its ability to conquer corners with absolute ease"

Back To The Future

The F430 features a host of styling cues from Ferrari's rich heritage – the air scoops at the rear pay homage to the 250 LM's, and the two elliptical air intakes at the front are inspired by Ferrari's 1961 F1 racing cars. Even the wing mirrors are similar to the Testarossa of the 1980s. Of course, the Enzo heavily influences the rear layout – the only elements that have remained from the 360 to the F430 are the doors, bonnet and roof.

Wind Up

The F430 is undeniably a beautiful car but, as with any serious supercar, the form follows function. The development of the F430 saw Ferrari's engineers spending over 2,000 hours in a wind tunnel making sure that the aerodynamics of the car were honed to perfection.

A Big Downer

The F430 features a 50 percent increase in downforce when compared to its successor, the 360 Modena. That means stability and safety at high speeds is now vastly improved.

Devil In The Details

Ferrari want owners to bespoke the F430 to their hearts content. Not only can customers turn up with a colour sample that they want their car painted in but they can also decide on the tiny details, such as the thread colour used inside the car and even the spacing of the actual stitching.

Ferrari F430: The Specifications

ENGINE	Aluminium V8	STEERING	Rack & pinion with power assist		adjustable tube shocks & anti-roll bar
VALVETRAIN	DOHC, 4 valves / cyl with variable timing and variable intake tract	BRAKES FRONT	Carbon-ceramic discs (optional) with 6-piston callipers / 380mm/15in, ABS, EBD	SUSPENSION REAR	Double wishbones with coil springs, electrically adjustable tube shocks & anti-roll bar
DISPLACEMENT	4308cc				
MAXIMUM POWER	483bhp at 8,500rpm				
MAXIMUM TORQUE	343lb ft at 5,250rpm	BRAKES REAR	Carbon-ceramic discs (optional), 4-piston callipers/350mm/14in, ABS, EBD	KERB WEIGHT	1450kg/3197lbs
TRANSMISSION	Six-speed manual (optional F1 paddleshift available)			LENGTH	4512mm/178in
				WIDTH	1923mm/76in
				HEIGHT	1214mm/48in
0–60MPH	4secs	SUSPENSION FRONT	Double wishbones with coil springs, electrically	WHEELS FRONT	7.5 x 19in
MAXIMUM SPEED	196mph			WHEEL REAR	10 x 19in

Ford GT

The Ferrari-beating Le Mans racing legend is reborn and the motoring world falls in love all over again...

The GT40's legacy was talked about for decades to come. But fast forward to the Detroit Auto Show, USA, in 2002 – where the concept of its successor is unveiled – and everyone starts talking again. The world does a double take, pinches itself to make sure that it isn't dreaming and then scrabbles for its chequebook.

Sitting close to the ground on its low profile tyres, the GT epitomizes how a proper sports car should look and, with a Ford-claimed 500bhp nestled behind the driver, how it should go as well. With a 0–60 time of 3.7secs and a top speed of 200mph, this is no lukewarm or cynical attempt to cash-in on Ford's heritage.

The GT may look dimensionally like the original at first glance but the car is actually 84mm/3.3in taller than its forbearer, and it's wider. And underneath that fine looking exterior is a thoroughly modern all-aluminium spaceframe. Providing the fireworks is a supercharged 5.4-litre V8 mid-engine lump with enough torque to rip tarmac from the road. Or at the very least, rip the rubber off those 19in tyres on the back. After all, the Ford features no traction control or fancy stability systems; driver and passenger air bags and anti-lock brakes are the only concessions to modern 'safe' motoring.

The car is renowned for being an absolute cinch to drive through rush hour as well as at full speed. Unlike some of its more 'highly strung' supercar competitors, this car also enjoys being on the limit, and with the GT's chassis, spot-on steering and entertaining handling, has the driving experience to match those damn fine looks too.

"*The original GT40 was a beautiful car; but the Ford GT is quite simply stunning*"

As Good As Old

Like the exterior, the GT's cockpit is a modern take on the old GT40 featuring toggle switches, seats with ventilated seat backs and squabs, and a speedo located above the transmission tunnel.

Fast Forward

To make sure that the GT was ready for their centennial celebrations in 2003, Ford managed to turn the concept car into a production model in a record-breaking 16 months.

Last In Line

Of the 5,000 GTs made, Ford allowed only 85 cars to be shipped over to Europe. The poor old UK had only 24 allocated – so you can only begin to imagine the scrambling of potential purchasers as they tried to get on the fabled shortlist.

The Past Made New

The GT is actually part of Ford's Living Legends range – cars from yester-year given a fresh reworking. Other cars in the series include the glorious-looking Ford Mustang and Thunderbird.

Size Matters

The original GT40 was named so because it was 1016mm/40in tall. The GT has crept up in height to accommodate taller drivers and now stands at 1100mm/43.3in. The height difference aside, if you're wondering why Ford didn't simply stick with GT40 as the name, well, it's because they don't actually own the copyright to it.

Ford GT: The Specifications

ENGINE	Aluminium V8	STEERING	Rack & pinion with power assist		adjustable tube shocks & anti-roll bar
VALVETRAIN	DOHC, 4 valves / cyl with variable timing and variable intake tract	BRAKES FRONT	Carbon-ceramic discs (optional) with 6-piston callipers / 380mm/15in, ABS, EBD	SUSPENSION REAR	Double wishbones with coil springs, electrically adjustable tube shocks & anti-roll bar
DISPLACEMENT	4308cc				
MAXIMUM POWER	483bhp at 8,500rpm				
MAXIMUM TORQUE	343lb ft at 5,250rpm	BRAKES REAR	Carbon-ceramic discs (optional), 4-piston callipers/350mm/14in, ABS, EBD	KERB WEIGHT	1450kg/3197lbs
TRANSMISSION	Six-speed manual (optional F1 paddleshift available)			LENGTH	4512mm/178in
				WIDTH	1923mm/76in
				HEIGHT	1214mm/48in
0–60MPH	4secs	SUSPENSION FRONT	Double wishbones with coil springs, electrically	WHEELS FRONT	7.5 x 19in
MAXIMUM SPEED	196mph			WHEEL REAR	10 x 19in

Ford GT (2003)

Ford GT40
(1966 Le Mans)

Honda NSX

A supercar? From Japan? If you think that only the Europeans make supercars, think again. Honda has been producing one of the world's finest for the past 15 years...

The mid-engined, rear-wheel drive aluminium-bodied NSX is remarkable. Designed with extensive help from the world's greatest Formula One driver, Ayrton Senna, the car was launched in 1990 to critical acclaim.

As with all Honda VTECs, using the full range of the engine rewards the driver with a frenzy of power the higher up the rev range they go. This power delivery is coupled with a rewarding chassis that offers huge grip and balance.

While exotic supercars can demand deep pockets for unexpected 'temperamental' breakdowns, the NSX is Japanese. Honda know how to screw a car together whether it be a 1.4 Civic or a 276bhp supercar.

The current NSX was introduced in 2002 and has seen the original's pop-up headlamps replaced by fixed headlamps. The current car also has two engines to choose from – the 3.2-litre V6 with a six-speed manual producing 276bhp, and the 3-litre V6 F-Matic version that produces 256bhp.

"The NSX – designed with extensive help from the world's greatest Formula One driver, Ayrton Senna"

Senna Sense

While Ayrton Senna was over in Japan in 1989, he was asked to drive a prototype of the original NSX to glean his expert thoughts. According to Honda, he told their engineers: "I'm not sure I can really give you appropriate advice on a mass-production car, but I feel it's a little fragile". Because of that input, the Honda team ended up increasing the car's rigidity by 50 percent.

Going Topless

The NSX is available with a targa top roof as well – the NSX-T – but critics do say that this affects the car's rigidity and that purists should stick to the coupé version.

World First

The NSX was the first production car in the world to feature all-aluminium construction for the chassis, suspension components and chassis, and it is still the only true mid-engine two-seater supercar to come out of the Land of the Rising Sun.

Fighting Talk

The NSX's sleek looks have their origins in the air, not on the road. The original sketches drawn up for the supercar were actually based on an F16 fighter jet.

Hand-Assembled Heaven

The NSX is hand-assembled in Japan. To make sure the engineers are good enough to put together the supercar, they have to go through a rigorous testing process before being allowed to work on the NSX.

Honda NSX Coupe 3.2 V6 / Acura NSX: The Specifications

ENGINE	24-valve V6	STEERING	Rack and pinion with Servotronic speed-sensitive power-assist	SUSPENSION REAR	Double wishbones with monutube dampers, coil springs & anti-roll bar
VALVETRAIN	DOHC VTEC 4 valves / cyl				
DISPLACEMENT	3179cc				
MAXIMUM POWER	276bhp at 7,300rpm	BRAKES FRONT	Ventilated & grooved with six callipers/ 355mm/14in	KERB WEIGHT	1710kg/3770lbs (manual) 1800kg/3968lbs (auto)
MAXIMUM TORQUE	220lb ft at 5,300rpm				
TRANSMISSION	Six-speed manual or six-speed Auto			LENGTH	4430mm/174in
		BRAKES REAR	Ventilated & grooved with 4 callipers/ 330mm/13in	WIDTH	1810mm/71in
0–60MPH	5.7secs (manual) 4.9secs (auto)			HEIGHT	1160mm/46in
				WHEELS FRONT	7 x 17in
0–100MPH	4.9secs (manual) 5.1secs (auto)	SUSPENSION FRONT	Double wishbones with monutube dampers, coil springs & anti-roll bar	WHEEL REAR	9 x 17in
MAXIMUM SPEED	168mph				

Koenigsegg CC

Ferociously fast, perfectly composed and luxurious... ladies and gentlemen, meet Sweden's McLaren F1 slayer with the world's most unpronounceable name...

Made in Sweden, the Koenigsegg CC, the dark horse of the supercar world, first broke cover in 2000, the car is the brainchild of Christian von Koenigsegg who set up the supercar project back in 1993 with a small, dedicated group of enthusiasts.

With its latest incarnations, the CC8S and the CCR, that power is now the stuff of legend – the top of the range CCR is officially the fastest

production car in the world and can propel you to McLaren F1-vanquishing speeds of beyond 242mph. The chassis, made from carbon fibre composite, is renowned for its communicative feedback whether the car's hurtling along at 200mph plus, or being threaded through pot-holed city streets.

While the 'base' model – the CC8S – offers 655bhp, its big brother, the

CCR launched in 2004, has a staggering 806bhp on tap and can make the dash from 0–62 in only 3.2secs. This 'extreme' version of the Koenigsegg is achieved by boosting the 'standard' 4.7-litre V8 engine with a bi-compressor centrifugal supercharging system.

As well as a full leather interior and CD player, the driver can indulge in luxuries such as GPS navigation, a rear-view camera, a telephone system and even bespoke suitcases. Open-air thrills are also available because the car comes with a removable roof panel that can be stored under the front bonnet.

Yes, the price tag of £407,000 plus (US price based on customer specification) is a huge amount of cash – but the Koenigsegg is worth every penny.

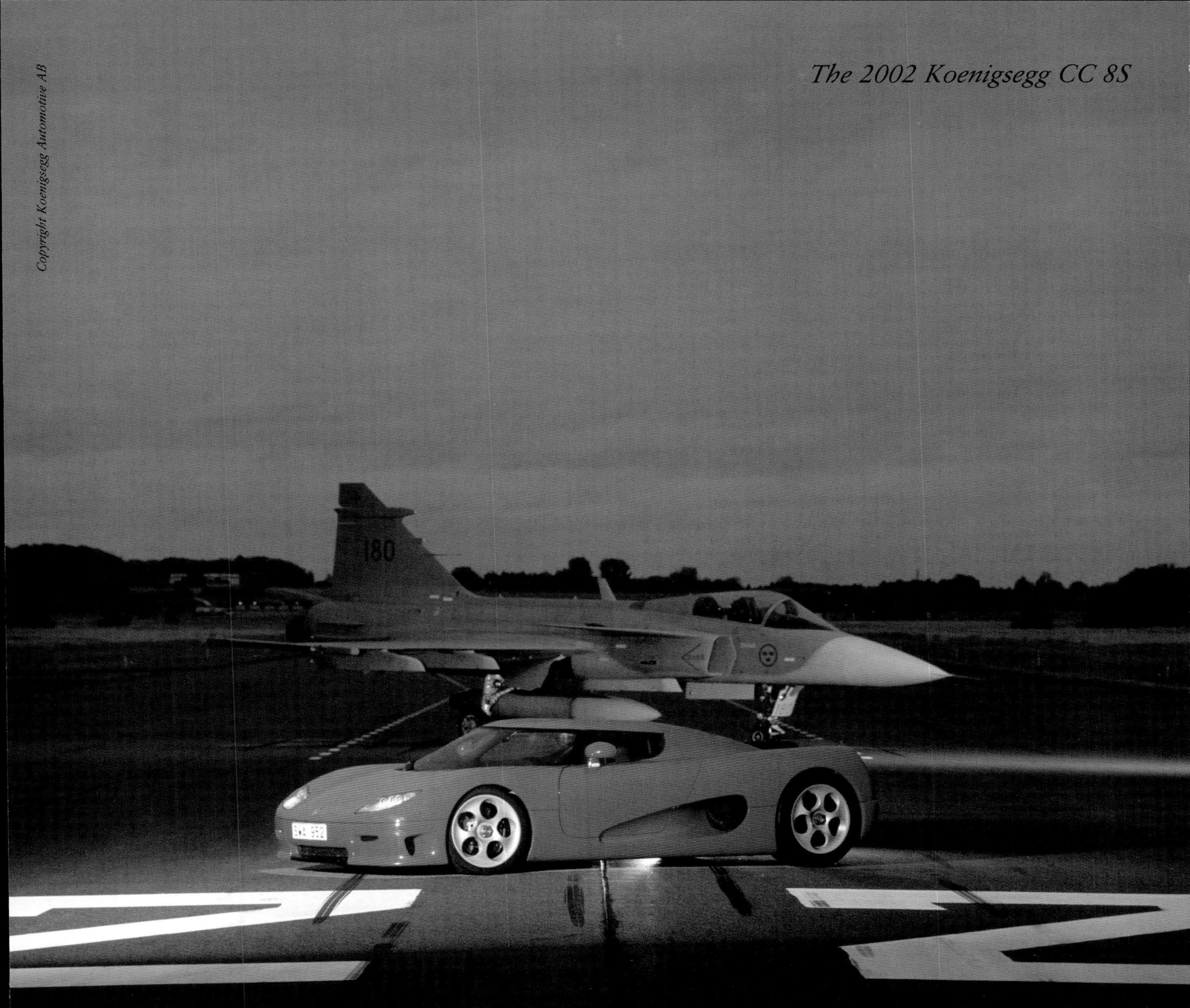

The 2002 Koenigsegg CC 8S

"*A truly remarkable supercar and virtually unbeatable; never has the phrase 'from zero to hero' been quite so true*"

Full House

The Koenigsegg headquarters are housed in a large fighter jet facility and there are 30 full-time staff. At the moment, seven vehicles can be assembled simultaneously and one car – bearing in mind there are 300-plus carbon fibre parts per car – takes 1,000 hours to assemble.

Door To Door

The carbon fibre doors of the CC open by swinging upwards and resting at a 90° angle. Thanks to gas struts, this operation can be done with a gentle push and also means that the car is easily accessible even in confined spaces.

Record Breaker

In the 2004 edition of the Guinness Book Of Records, the Koenigsegg CC8S is listed as the most powerful production car on the face of the planet. This has now been smashed by the 806bhp CCR.

Have Car, Wheel Travel

The five-spoke magnesium alloy rims featured on the CCR have been specifically designed for Koenigsegg, and the tyres are guaranteed to withstand the strains and stresses of travelling at over 240mph.

Not Too Hot To Handle?

The engineers at Koenigsegg have implemented KACS (Koenigsegg Advanced Control System) as standard on the CCR – this allows the driver to adjust the car's suspension, aerodynamics, road holding and braking.

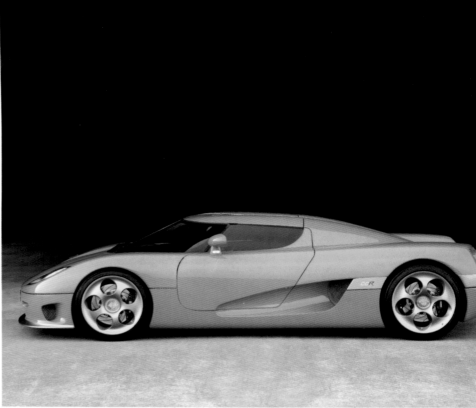

Koenigsegg CCR: The Specifications

ENGINE	V8 cast aluminium, supercharged	**BRAKES FRONT**	Ventilated with six-piston light alloy callipers, ABS/362mm/14in
VALVETRAIN	DOHC 4 valves / cyl		
DISPLACEMENT	4700cc	**BRAKES REAR**	Ventilated with six-piston callipers/362mm/14in
MAXIMUM POWER	806bhp at 6,900rpm		
MAXIMUM TORQUE	678lb ft at 5,700rpm	**SUSPENSION FRONT**	Double wishbones, adjustable VPS custom racing shock absorbers, pushrod operated & anti-roll bar
TRANSMISSION	Six-speed manual		
0–60MPH	5.9secs		
0–100MPH	11.9secs		
MAXIMUM SPEED	242mph +		
STEERING	Rack and pinion with power assist		

SUSPENSION REAR	Double wishbones, adjustable VPS custom racing shock absorbers, pushrod operated & anti-roll bar
KERB WEIGHT	1230kg/2711lb
LENGTH	4190mm/164in
WIDTH	1990mm/78in
HEIGHT	1070mm/42in
WHEELS FRONT	9.5 x 19in
WHEEL REAR	12.5 x 20in

Lamborghini Murcielago

German build quality partnered with Italian passion... it's an intriguing concept but one that has paid off for the raging bull...

While Audi has ensured that the car has improved safety features and is better built than its predecessors, the Murcielago still has more than enough go to put a cold sweat on the foreheads of even the most experienced driver when taking the car to the limit.

The engine alone will see to that – with 580bhp, the aluminium 6.2-litre V12 is blisteringly quick, and with its four-wheel drive with a central vicious coupler plus traction control, the steel and carbon fibre-built Lamborghini's huge power can be placed down on the road with more ease than its predecessors. The Murcielago also represents a first for the Lamborghini with the inclusion of a six-speed manual gearbox.

The car's rear spoiler adjusts depending on the speed, and those fabulous air intakes mounted on the car's rear shoulders open and close to cool the mammoth engine. And for the show-offs, there's also a dash-mounted button to activate that 'Variable Air-flow Cooling System'.

While the aggressive, melodramatic styling of previous Lamborghinis looked like testosterone wrought in metal, the more subtle Murcielago still demands your attention with its clean, simple and muscular lines – it's a thoroughly modern reimagining of the Lamborghini spirit penned by Belgian designer Luc Donckerwolcke.

It's with this new mindset – the passion of Lamborghini and the build quality of Audi – that the company has matured into a true 21st century supercar marque.

"*The Murcielago demands your attention with its clean, simple and muscular lines. It's a thoroughly modern reimagining of the Lamborghini spirit*"

What's In A Name?

The Murcielago is named after a bull that fought with the famous matador Rafael Molina 'Lagartijo' on October 5, 1879. The aforementioned bull fought so bravely – and withstood being stabbed 24 times – that the great matador decided to honor the bull and spare its life. The bull was given to a top breeder and the Murcielago lineage continues to this day.

Bullet Proof?

Build quality and reliability were issues that sometimes hovered over the Lamborghinis of old. The now Audi-owned company say that Murcielagos are being driven over 10,000 miles a year by some customers with no problems.

Off With Its Head

Unlike the Diablo Roadster, which horrified the critics on its release, the Murcielago Roadster has taken their breaths away – not only incredible to look at but also a true zero-compromise supercar as well.

All-Wheel Thrills

Lamborghini wanted all the Murcielago's power put firmly down on the road so the driver could enjoy it, and not simply destroy the car's tyres. Subsequently, any excess torque on the rear axle is moved to the front axle to aid the Murcielago get the best traction.

Lamborghini Murcielago: The Specifications

ENGINE	Aluminium alloy V12	0–125MPH	8.6secs	SUSPENSION REAR	Double wishbones with
VALVETRAIN	DOHC, 4 valves / cyl	MAXIMUM SPEED	205mph		coil springs, gas dampers
	with variable-geometry	STEERING	Rack & Pinion with		& anti-roll bar
	intake system and variable		power assist	KERB WEIGHT	1650kg/3638lbs
	valve timing	BRAKES FRONT	Vented discs with 4-pot	LENGTH	4580mm/180in
DISPLACEMENT	6192cc		callipers, ABS/355mm/14in	WIDTH	2045mm/80in
MAXIMUM POWER	580bhp at 7,500rpm	BRAKES REAR	Vented Discs with 4-pot	HEIGHT	1135mm/45in
MAXIMUM TORQUE	479lb ft at 5,400rpm		callipers, ABS/335mm	WHEELS FRONT	8.5 x 18in
TRANSMISSION	Six-speed manual /	SUSPENSION FRONT	Double wishbones with	WHEEL REAR	13 x 18in
	Optional E-Gear		coil springs, gas dampers		
0–60MPH	3.8secs		& anti-roll bar		

Lamborghini Gallardo

So, you can't stretch to a Murcielago? There's no need to worry because its baby brother is just as convincing...

That commute has never been quite so much fun – indeed, this car is easy to manage in the chaos of the rush hour but like any Lamborghini, the Gallardo is designed to be

pushed, and heavy-footing the accelerator shows that this bull hasn't lost its horns. That V10 bellows its way up the rev range, easily managed with the six-speed manual or the optional e-Gear sequential gear shifting system that lets the driver flick through the paddles mounted on the steering column.

This power is delivered by a mid-mounted V10 5-litre engine, which produces 493bhp. The

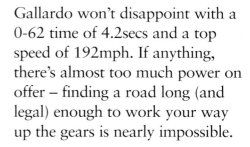

Gallardo won't disappoint with a 0-62 time of 4.2secs and a top speed of 192mph. If anything, there's almost too much power on offer – finding a road long (and legal) enough to work your way up the gears is nearly impossible.

With its fully adjustable, electrically operated leather seats, there are enough creature comforts, such as air-conditioning and even optional satellite navigation, for the long-distance driver. The only blot on the landscape is actually accessing that cabin, which may disappoint if you are expecting scissor doors that sweep elegantly up into the air. No, these are, dare we say, just hinged conventional doors.

What's most striking about the Gallardo is just how successful Lamborghini has been at muscling its way into traditional Ferrari territory without any compromise in Lamborghini's philosophy.

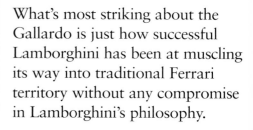

"The Gallardo is designed to be pushed, and heavy-footing the accelerator shows that this bull hasn't lost its horns"

Winging It

The Gallardo's rear wing is able to change its angle depending on how quickly the car is moving. Below 50mph, the wing remains flush with the rest of the Gallardo's bodywork but at 80mph, it shifts upwards to create more downforce. After all, with 500bhp, the Gallardo needs all the stability it can get.

The Lamborghini A8?

Audi didn't just stipulate the Gallardo's build quality, they also lent their air-conditioning system and stereo; you can normally find them residing in the Audi A8. This might be a cost-cutting exercise for Lamborghini but, at the end of the day, both of the Audi elements are of a very high quality, so Gallardo owners needn't be disappointed.

Instant Hit

It's a blessing for any keen driver who's just taken delivery of their new pride and joy – unlike many cars, the Gallardo's engine needs no 'breaking-in' period before unleashing the car's huge potential. To ensure that drivers can start wringing the most out of the V10's huge power, the engine is actually run in at the factory before being mounted in the Gallardo.

Lamborghini Gallardo: The Specifications

ENGINE	Aluminium V10	0–125MPH	9.0secs		springs, dampers &
VALVETRAIN	DOHC, 4 valves / cyl	MAXIMUM SPEED	192mph		anti-roll bar
	with variable intake	STEERING	Rack and pinion with	SUSPENSION REAR	Double wishbones
	system & continuously		power assist		w/anti-roll bar with coil
	variable valve timing	BRAKES FRONT	Ventilated discs with 8-		springs, dampers &
DISPLACEMENT	4961cc		piston callipers/365mm/		anti-roll bar
MAXIMUM POWER	493bhp at 7,800rpm		14in, ABS	KERB WEIGHT	1530kg/3373lbs
MAXIMUM TORQUE	376Ib ft at 4,500 rpm	BRAKES REAR	Ventilated discs with 8-	LENGTH	4300mm/169in
TRANSMISSION	Six-speed manual		piston callipers/335mm/	WIDTH	1900mm/75in
	(optional E-gear		14in, ABS	HEIGHT	1165mm/46in
	system available)	SUSPENSION FRONT	Double wishbones	WHEELS FRONT	8.5 x 19in
0–60MPH	4.2secs		w/anti-roll bar with coil	WHEEL REAR	11 x 19in

Maserati MC12

*The car you're looking at is a Ferrari Enzo.
Well, it isn't. But it is. Let us explain...*

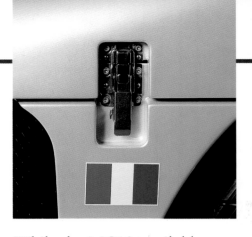

Up until recently, Maserati was in partnership with Ferrari and thanks to the Italian stallion, the MC12 has its engineering roots in the legendary Ferrari Enzo. It features the same carbon monocoque, the same V12 engine (albeit detuned), and even the same basic steering wheel and windshield. But the MC12 is aerodynamically superior to the prancing horse. After all, it's 610mm/24in longer and it features extended overhangs at both the back and rear. That means the engineers have been able to optimise how the air flows over (and exits) the MC12's body.

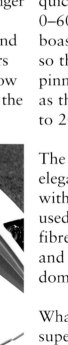

While the MC12 available to the public isn't the actual car that will race round tracks scooping up awards, it's close enough. Hit the accelerator and any illusions of being in a user-friendly runabout vanish quicker than the car hitting 0–60 in 3.8secs. The MC12 boasts an even power delivery so the driver is constantly pinned back in his racing seat as the car thunders its way up to 205mph.

The interior of the MC12 is an elegant but functional cockpit with lightweight carbon fibre used in abundance. The carbon fibre seats feature full harnesses, and a large rev counter dominates the MC12's dials.

What's incredible about this supercar is what Masearti managed to achieve in 12 months – it's nothing short of a miracle.

*"The Maserati
MC12 has its
engineering roots
in the legendary
Ferrari Enzo"*

Long Time Coming
Maserati, a name synonymous with racing excellence, achieved its last victory way back in 1967 with the Cooper Maserati F1 at the South African Grand Prix.

Design Guru
While the MC12 was built for functionality rather than creative form, the supercar still has the kind of road presence that shames many of its competitors – it was designed by Frank Stephenson whose last job before joining up with the Ferrari Maserati Group was to design the Mini Cooper.

What's In A Colour?
The MC12 is available only in a two-tone white and blue livery. This colour scheme is in homage to the Maserati Tipo 60–61 'Birdcages' from the early 1960s.

Keeping Up With The Jones'es
The MC12 is surely the last word in exclusivity – only 50 will ever be made.

Hooked On Air
Like a true Le Mans racer, the MC12 features a large snorkel on its roof and rear grille to shove air down on to the Ferrari Enzo-sourced V12 engine.

Speedy Production
It's claimed that to get the MC12 from the drawing board to the finished car took a year. In fact, every element of creating the car was done at light speed – the alloys took a mere 15 days to go from design to the prototype wheel.

Maserati MC12: The Specifications

ENGINE	V12	BRAKES FRONT	Cross-drilled & ventilated discs with 6-piston callipers,ABS/380mm/15in	SUSPENSION REAR	Double wishbones with push-rod links, steel dampers & coil springs
VALVETRAIN	DOHC, 4 valves / cyl				
DISPLACEMENT	5998cc				
MAXIMUM POWER	622bhp at 7,500rpm	BRAKES REAR	Cross-drilled & ventilated discs with 4-piston callipers, ABS/335mm/13in	KERB WEIGHT	1335kg/2943lbs
MAXIMUM TORQUE	480lb ft at 5,500rpm			LENGTH	5143mm/202in
TRANSMISSION	Six-speed sequential manual			WIDTH	2096mm/82in
		SUSPENSION FRONT	Double wishbones with push-rod links, steel dampers & coil springs	HEIGHT	1205mm/47in
0–60MPH	3.8secs			WHEELS FRONT	9 x 19in
MAXIMUM SPEED	205mph			WHEEL REAR	13 x 19in
STEERING	Rack and pinion with power assist				

Mercedes-Benz McLaren SLR

The three-pointed star wanted to make an impact with their first true supercar. Here's how they pulled it off...

Like its forefather, the new SLR pushes out the technological envelope too – a process helped by teaming up with their Formula One partners, McLaren, who are rather well known for producing what is arguably still the greatest supercar of all time – the McLaren F1.

Just look over the long dart-like form of the car and its arrow-shaped nose, and it's not hard to see how the SLR's design elements are clearly inspired by the Formula One Silver Arrows. That full carbon fibre body encases cutting edge mechanics – a hand-assembled supercharged 5.5-litre V8 engine, producing 626bhp (and enough torque to beat its chief rival, the Ferrari Enzo) is mounted towards the front of the chassis. Power delivery is borderline insane.

The only chink in the SLR's formidable armour is its ceramic brakes – they've been regularly criticized for their complete lack of feel, leaving the driver having to learn how to use the SLR's electronically regulated braking power – not something that you particularly want to do in a supercar that can hit 0–60 in 3.7secs.

Opening the gull wing doors of the SLR reveals a snug interior - an optional claret-red leather-swathed interior can be ordered, a colour arrangement inspired by the 1950s SLR's interior. Electronically adjustable carbon-frame seats, chronometer-style instruments and the use of carbon fibre and aluminium create an environment that should see drivers happily clocking up hundreds of miles in style.

"The new SLR is a classic, managing to straddle the gap between the ferocious performance of a supercar and the luxuries of a GT"

Smooth Operator

Based on Formula One technology, the SLR's underbody is virtually smooth. That coupled with a six-channel diffuser at the rear means that there is minimal drag and more downforce produced when hitting higher speeds. Even the exhausts have been moved to the side to ensure that aerodynamics aren't affected – those sidepipes also pay tribute to those featured on the 1950s SLR.

Sudden Impact

If an SLR driver should find themselves about to go nose first into an immovable object, they can seek solace in the car's long carbon fibre body and front end crash structure, offering the kind of energy absorption in crashes that has saved many lives on the Formula One circuit.

Acronym Explained

During the SLR's heyday in the 1950s, the SLR stood for Sporty Light Racer.

"How do I start this?"

The SLR has the obligatory starter button. Instead of being mounted in the central console, the glowing red starter button is actually located on the end of the gear lever – simply flip back the cover and push down.

Geared For Action

The five-speed auto gearbox sourced from the Mercedes-owned luxury limo, the Maybach, comes with two automatic settings and three manual ones. The manual settings can be accessed via the gear lever or the steering wheel-mounted buttons.

Mercedes-Benz SLR: The Specifications

ENGINE	AMG V8	**STEERING**	Rack & pinion with power assist	**SUSPENSION FRONT**	Double wishbones with coil springs & gas dampers
VALVETRAIN	SOHC, 3 valves / cyl				
DISPLACEMENT	5439cc	**BRAKES FRONT**	Fibre reinforced ceramic discs with eight piston callipers, ESP, SBC/ 370mm/14.5in		
MAXIMUM POWER	626bhp at 6,500rpm			**SUSPENSION REAR**	Double wishbones with coil springs & gas dampers
MAXIMUM TORQUE	575lb ft at 3250– 5000rpm				
TRANSMISSION	5-Speed Auto with Speedshift System	**BRAKES REAR**	Fibre reinforced ceramic discs with 4 piston callipers, ESP, SBC/360mm/14in	**KERB WEIGHT**	1768kg/3898lbs
				LENGTH	4656mm/183in
0–60MPH	3.7secs			**WIDTH**	1908mm/75in
0–125MPH	10.7secs			**HEIGHT**	1261mm/50in
MAXIMUM SPEED	208mph			**WHEELS FRONT**	9 x 18in
				WHEEL REAR	11.5 x 18in

Mitsubishi Lancer Evolution VIII 400

Copyright Mitsubishi Motors Ltd

While supercars can trace their DNA back to the race track, the Evo range was born out of the mud, gravel and pot holes of rallying...

The Evo VIII FQ-400 can produce a G-force that would give the sort of Hollywood facelift that an aging actress would kill for. In the 3.5secs it takes to hit 60mph, the trouble is that it could also age you if you're not up to handling the Evo's huge power.

While the FQ-400 may be easy to handle driving round town at low revs, hit the magic power band at 5,000rpm, and the turbo kicks in properly. Once the turbo is churning out its power through the rally-sourced four-wheel drive, you won't be able to believe that it's all coming from a 2-litre turbo-charged engine. This car produces a whopping 405bhp.

With neutral handling, tidy body control and colossal grip, the Evo can devour corners with unnerving confidence. Many argue though that the FQ-400 is simply too extreme and that FQ-340 version will give you great performance but of the sort that can be used more frequently on the average trip to the supermarket.

Remember that this is a Japanese car so reliability comes as standard – but this extreme engineering of the Evo has the benefit of being backed-up by a cast-iron three year/36,000 miles warranty – that even includes drivers who've taken to tearing their Evos round tracks on a regular basis.

Copyright Mitsubishi Motors Ltd

WX54
MFZ

"Being a rally car designed for the road, the Evo can do the twisty stuff as well as the 0–100mph assault on your senses. With neutral handling, tidy body control and colossal grip, the Evo can devour corners with unnerving confidence"

107

Frightfully Quick

The MR stands for 'Mitsubishi Racing' but ever wondered what the FQ in the MR FQ-400 stands for?

Number Crunching...

The Pagani Zonda cranks out a very respectable 76.12bhp per litre. The Porsche Carrera GT manages 106.75. The FQ-400 claims 202.5bhp per litre.

Need For FQ Speed

The FQ-400 is not only the fastest road-going car that Mitsubishi has ever made (for the UK market at least) – it also has the honour of being the fastest accelerating four-door sedan, from a major manufacturer, ever to grace public roads.

Ready To Launch

To keep the FQ-400's immense power welded to the road, instead of coming off at the first corner, Mitsubishi's engineers have made sure that the car remains stable at high speeds with the inclusion of a carbon fibre front lip spoiler, Ralliart aero mirrors and the rather menacing rear vortex generator – the 'shark's teeth' that can be found poking out of the rear of the roof.

So Little, So Much

Just how did Mitsubishi manage to get so much brake horse power out of a 2-litre engine? The most important element is the Garrett turbocharger made especially for the FQ-400, and the engine has also been strengthened to withstand the huge forces needed to develop 405bhp.

Mitsubishi Lancer Evo VIII MR FQ-400: The Specifications

ENGINE	Inline-4	**BRAKES FRONT**	Alcon 6-pot monobloc brake kit / 343mm/13in	**SUSPENSION REAR**	McPherson strut suspension with inverted shock absorbers, stabilizer bar & aluminium front lower arms
VALVETRAIN	DOHC turbo with intercooler	**BRAKES REAR**	Ventilated discs with 2-pot aluminium callipers/300mm/12in		
DISPLACEMENT	1997cc				
MAXIMUM POWER	405bhp at 6,400rpm	**SUSPENSION FRONT**	McPherson strut suspension with inverted shock absorbers, stabilizer bar & aluminium front lower arms	**KERB WEIGHT**	1400kg/3086lbs
MAXIMUM TORQUE	355lb ft at 5,500rpm			**LENGTH**	4490mm/177in
TRANSMISSION	Six-speed manual			**WIDTH**	1770mm/70in
0–60MPH	3.5secs			**HEIGHT**	1450mm/57in
0–100MPH	9.1secs			**WHEELS FRONT**	8 x 17in
MAXIMUM SPEED	175mph			**WHEEL REAR**	8 x 17in
STEERING	Rack and pinion with power assist				

Pagani Zonda

-Exotic, outlandish, eccentric... the Zonda is the most individual supercar the world has ever seen...

First revealed at the Geneva Motor Show, Switzerland, in 1999, the prototype of the Zonda was always going to cause a fuss – with those alien looks, it simply couldn't fail not to. At the heart of the car is its unique use of composite materials with a carbon fibre chassis and body, ensuring an incredibly lightweight and rigid structure. Add into that a bullet-proof, smooth-revving Mercedes-Benz AMG V12 – after all, those Germans know how to build a reliable engine that won't blow up when you're attempting to top 200mph. The original five-speed C12 had 389bhp on tap in 6.9-litre form and has been constantly evolving ever since. The six-speed Zonda C12 S which is shown here has now evolved into the S 7.3 – all 555bhp of it boasting a 0–60 time of 3.6secs. Traction control is included, which is mighty handy for nailing all that power to the road in wet conditions.

Perhaps the most keenly anticipated Pagani was the 555bhp Roadster – but there was a genuine concern among fans that chopping off the roof of the Zonda would leave its handling horribly compromised. But again, Pagani and his team managed to blow away any concerns by introducing a new carbon fibre central chassis structure, and a roll bar made from carbon and chrome-molybdene to ensure that rigidity remained at the heart of the Zonda Roadster's winning formula.

The most extreme Zonda was introduced in 2005 – the F version. Built alongside the standard Zonda, it features a lighter chassis and better aerodynamics courtesy of a host of changes including a larger front splitter. That monster Mercedes engine is now even more powerful thanks to a new induction system which means you've got a whopping 602bhp under your right foot – the power-hungry driver wanting even more acceleration can of course settle for the Clubsport edition that boasts 650bhp.

"The Zonda was always going to cause a fuss. With those alien looks, it simply couldn't fail not to"

Exclusivity Guaranteed
The Roadster is regarded as the most desirable of the Zonda range, so interested customers are recommended to put their Roadster's production will be capped at only 40.

What's In A Name?
What's a supercar without a suitably evocative name? The word Zonda actually comes from a warm wind that blows west across the Andes Mountains in South America.

In Good Company
The Zonda's creator Horacio Pagani had expert help from the now-deceased Grand Prix racing legend, Juan Manuel Fangio. He is credited with aiding Horacio with all aspects of the supercar's creation – from its styling to its world-class handling.

Bespoke Heaven
The interior of the Zonda is as unique as its exterior with its mix of aluminium, leather and carbon fibre. Of course, for that special supercar touch, the company also provides owners with bespoke leather luggage and a pair of driving shoes with every car.

Leap Of Faith
Talk about conviction – Horacio Pagani was so sure that the Zonda would be a hit with the public once they'd seen it at the 1999 Geneva Motor Show, that he'd already had the car crash tested and ramped up ready for production.

Pagani Zonda S 7.3: The Specifications

ENGINE	V12	STEERING	Rack and pinion with power assist	SUSPENSION REAR	Double wishbones with helical springs, hydraulic dampers & anti-roll bar
VALVETRAIN	DOHC 4 valves / cyl				
DISPLACEMENT	7291cc	BRAKES FRONT	Ventilated with four-piston callipers, ABS/355mm/14in		
MAXIMUM POWER	555bhp at 5,900rpm			KERB WEIGHT	1350kg/2976lbs
MAXIMUM TORQUE	553lb ft at 4,050rpm	BRAKES REAR	Ventilated with four-piston callipers, ABS/355mm/14in	LENGTH	4395mm/173in
TRANSMISSION	Six-speed manual			WIDTH	2055mm/81in
0–60MPH	3.6secs	SUSPENSION FRONT	Double wishbones with helical springs, hydraulic dampers & anti-roll bar	HEIGHT	1151mm/45in
0–100MPH	Sub 8secs			WHEELS FRONT	9 x 18in
MAXIMUM SPEED	220mph			WHEEL REAR	13 x 18in

Porsche Carrera GT

Sports car maker Porsche had been out of the supercar game for nearly two decades. Trust them to come storming back onto the scene with a road racer that makes all the right noises...

It's been a long while coming – the last time Porsche unleashed anything resembling a true supercar on to the world stage was with the magnificent 959 back in 1987.

The GT's racing heritage is apparent throughout the car – it's got Formula One-style all-wishbone pushrod suspension, a brand new V10 engine (that was initially bound for Le Mans), and a small ceramic clutch that's mated to a six-speed manual transmission. Thanks to that diminutive clutch, it means the engine can be mounted lower in the car; the end result being better weight distribution and aerodynamics.

Unlike the normally rear-engined Porsches, the V10 is mounted in the middle and produces 612bhp. The low weight carbon fibre monocoque chassis coupled with such power means that the GT can do the 0–60 sprint in 3.8secs and 0–100 in a mere 6.9secs.

City driving needn't be a handful either with the car willing to idle along before you decide to floor the accelerator and be pushed back into the seat with its startling but ultimately progressive grunt – there are no nasty surprises awaiting the keen, experienced driver.

No one should be surprised that Porsche have managed to pull off a masterstroke with their supercar entry – the GT shows just what we've all been missing out on while Porsche has been in supercar hibernation. It's just a shame it took them so long to rejoin the party. Welcome back Porsche – we've missed you.

"On the twisty stuff, the GT comes into its own offering a benign drive that is all about feel and communication coupled with huge grip"

119

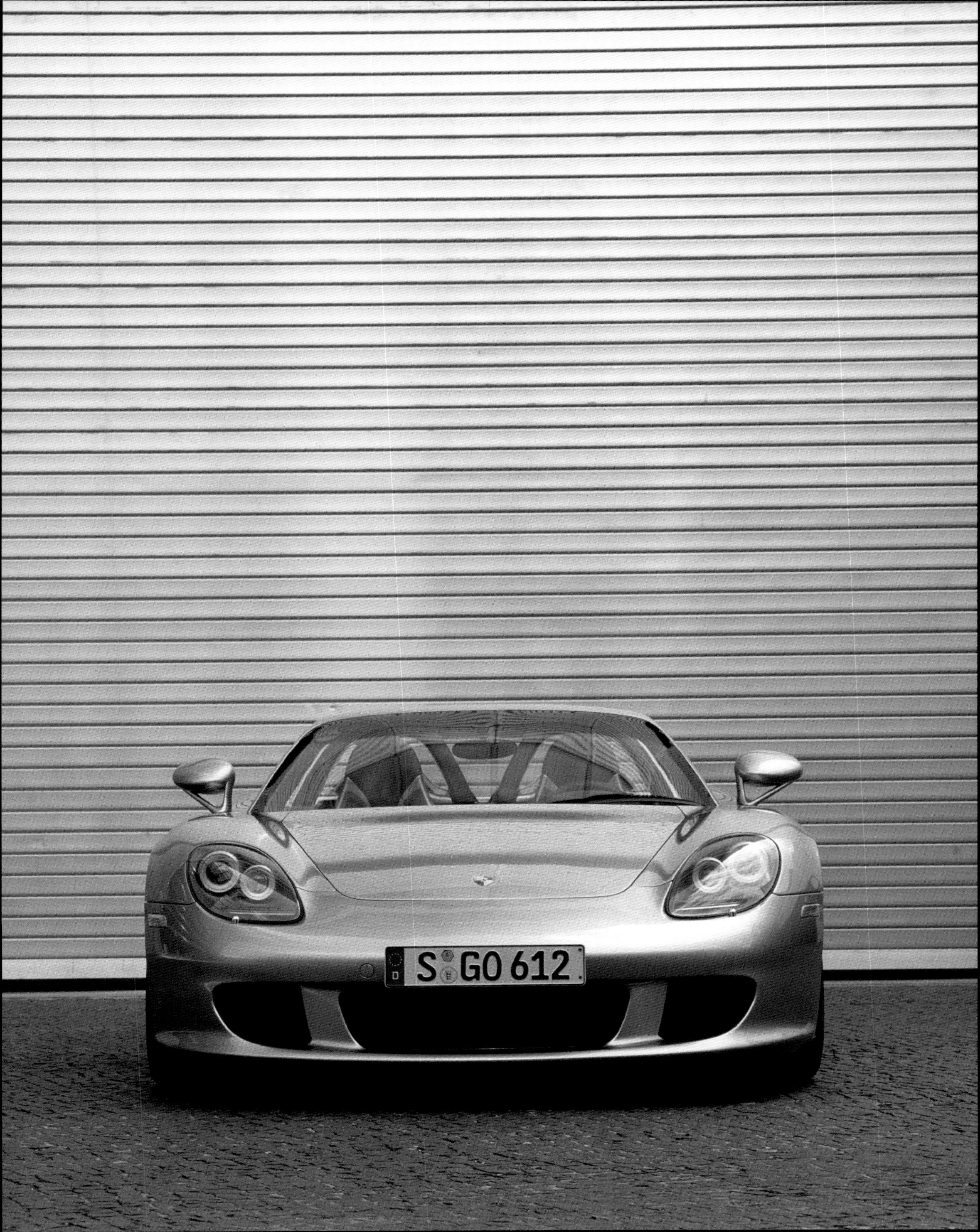
S GO 612

Touching Wood

A Porsche with a wood gear knob? It may seem out of place in a car that uses the latest composite materials, but that gear knob is a nod to the 1970–1971 Le Mans champ, the Porsche 917. So, why wood in the 917? Because it was the lightest material of that time – and it stopped the driver from scalding his hand when shifting gears.

Suited And Booted

There is space under the front bonnet for luggage in the GT but don't expect to be able to pack any kind of suitcase in there. In the meantime, Porsche provides a specially tailored travel bag to fit into the limited space.

Wheely, Wheely Good

To make a supercar, you have to be weight-obsessed – and Porsche is the 'supermodel' of supercars. For example, unlike most supercars that use aluminium alloy for their wheels, Porsche has used lighter forged magnesium. And those wheels need to be as light as possible – after all, they measure 19in at the front and a whopping 20in at the rear.

Perfect Service

Porsche claim that the GT requires the engine oil and air filter to be changed only every 12,000 miles; and the oil filter every 24,000 miles; and the spark plugs every four years or 24,000 miles.

Porsche Carrera GT: The Specifications

ENGINE	Aluminium V10	BRAKES FRONT	Porsche Ceramic Composite Brake (PCCB). Ventilated and cross-drilled with six-piston callipers, ABS/380mm/15in	SUSPENSION REAR	Double wishbones with inboard springs inc. dampers units
VALVETRAIN	DOHC 4 valves / cyl				
DISPLACEMENT	5733cc				
MAXIMUM POWER	612bhp at 8,000rpm			KERB WEIGHT	1380kg/3042lbs
MAXIMUM TORQUE	435lb ft at 5,750rpm			LENGTH	4,613mm/182in
TRANSMISSION	Six-speed manual with two-plate ceramic dry clutch	BRAKES REAR	Porsche Ceramic Composite Brake (PCCB). Ventilated and cross-drilled with six-piston callipers, ABS/380mm/15in	WIDTH	1,921mm/76in
				HEIGHT	1,166mm/46in
				WHEELS FRONT	9.5 x 19in
0–60MPH	3.8secs			WHEEL REAR	12.5 x 20in
0–100MPH	6.9secs				
MAXIMUM SPEED	205mph	SUSPENSION FRONT	Double wishbones with inboard springs inc. dampers units		
STEERING	Rack and pinion with power assist				

TVR Sagaris

It's loud; it's rude; it's not one for small talk, and it doesn't want to be everyone's friend... it's a TVR then...

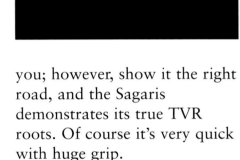

Look over the composite GRP bodywork of the TVR and your senses are assaulted from every angle – those dragon-esque headlamps, the mass of bonnet vents; and on the car's rump, well, have you ever seen a transparent rear spoiler? No, we thought not. Underneath, there's typical TVR firepower on offer for the brave-hearted driver. The Sagaris was intended to be a trackday car born out of the pretty TVR T350 that would also be suitable for road use; and with the finished car now bedazzling drivers, TVR has delivered on that promise.

With its 0-60 time of 3.7secs and 0-100 in 8.1secs, the 400bhp 4-litre engine mounted on the Sagaris's tubular steel chassis is easy to exploit with its five-speed gearbox. But for all its obvious drama, the Sagaris is day-to-day useable. While threading in and out of traffic, the car is not trying to scrabble to get away from

you; however, show it the right road, and the Sagaris demonstrates its true TVR roots. Of course it's very quick with huge grip.

Inside the Sagaris is equally special – two white dials peer out at the driver from the dashboard while the rest of the cabin is smothered in leather. Everything on view is bespoke – apart from the three-spoke steering wheel. You'll also notice the roll cage, there to 'reassure' anyone that while the car lacks electronic safety devices, you'll be well looked after if the worst does happen.

With its unmatched 'butch' charisma, no BS approach and obscene performance, the low volume British TVR range is something to be cherished; God bless the (melodrama) Queen.

"Visually, TVR doesn't do subtle, and the Sagaris is like being poked in the eye with an electric cattle prod. It's that shocking; it makes supercars such as the Ferrari F430 look everyday and hum-drum"

A Brief (Recent) History Of TVR

TVR was founded in 1947 – but in 2004, the company was sold to a 24-year-old entrepreneur, Nikolai Smolenski, who, at the last count, was worth nearly £55 million/US$105 million. His initial moves to take TVR into the 21st century have been to address the build quality issues that have plagued the handmade TVRs of the past; because customers have been put off by reliability issues, the Russian delayed the release of the Sagaris and the Tuscan 2 to ensure that build quality was improved.

Bound For The USA?

While TVR has amassed a cult following in the USA thanks to games such as PlayStation 2's Gran Turismo series and movies like Swordfish, the car isn't available to the US public. Only time will tell if the new owner of TVR has plans to unleash the brand in America.

"I'm A TV-R Star"

The Sagaris prototype unveiled to thrilled audiences in 2003 went on to become one of the stars of British reality TV show The Heist where ex-criminals were charged with the task of stealing it.
They succeeded.

Keeping It Close

The factory in Blackpool, England, makes practically everything you see inside and outside of a TVR, and the company's straight-six engines are the stuff of motoring legend.

Sagaris: The Specifications

NE	All-aluminium TVR Speed Six straight-six	STEERING	Rack and pinion with power assist	SUSPENSION REAR	Independent double wishbones with coils over gas hydraulic dampers & anti-roll bar
ACEMENT	3996cc	BRAKES FRONT	Ventilated discs with 4-piston alloy callipers/ 322mm/13in		
MUM POWER	406bhp at 7,000-7,500bhp			KERB WEIGHT	1078kg/2376lbs
MUM TORQUE	349lb ft at 5,000rpm	BRAKES REAR	Ventilated discs with single sliding piston callipers/298mm/12in	LENGTH	4057mm/160in
NSMISSION	Five-speed manual			WIDTH	1850mm/73in
PH	3.7secs			HEIGHT	1175mm/46in
PH	8.1secs	SUSPENSION FRONT	Independent double wishbones with coils over gas hydraulic dampers & anti-roll bar		
MUM SPEED	175mph				

TVR Tuscan 2

Now in its second generation, the Tuscan has 'grown up' to become a more civilized supercar than the hooligan-like original. But the beast still lurks beneath those strikingly beautiful looks...

Featuring TVR's incredible straight-six engine that produces a whopping 350bhp, the Tuscan 2 is blindingly fast – 0-60 takes 4.2secs, and the supercar will happily see 175mph and beyond. But TVR's engineers aren't known for sitting back and slapping themselves on the back for a job well down; they've been busy 'tinkering' and have produced the top of the range Tuscan 2 S that features 400bhp on tap and can hit 0-60 in 3.8secs – goodbye Gallardo. All that power is kept on the road at high speed thanks to a splitter under the front grille and a gurney above the boot lid which ensures downforce over both the front and rear axles.

Climb inside the TVR and the sight of a fully bespoke interior will greet you; all the vital readouts such as speed and revs are digital; the leather upholstery is made by TVR in-house, and the alloy switchgear is tactile and satisfying to use. There is an issue though for anyone familiar with the TVR brand – build quality.

The development of the TVR Tuscan 2 and the Sagaris though saw them being put through punishing conditions in Bahrain, South Africa, Saudi Arabia and Russia for the first time to ensure that the car could take high speeds in gruelling environments. Whether all the 'gremlins' have been wiped out remains to be seen though – only time will tell but with its three year/36,000 mile warranty, TVR is backing up its new found commitment to build quality with its bank balance.

"Driving a TVR on the limit requires focus and concentration, and there's precious little safety equipment on board if it all starts to go pear-shaped – no traction control, no ABS, no, well, anything – just an integrated roll-cage. The Tuscan's no pussycat but no TVR ever should be"

Doing It Differently

TVR is known for not playing by the rules with any element of its cars. They even have to do their doors differently – don't go looking for a traditional handle by the way; pushing a button underneath the wing mirror makes the window slip down, the door gently springing open. Now how's that for 'bespoke'?

Bark Worse Than Its Bite?

The TVR's straight-six engine sounds incredible – the deep roar that bellows every time you floor the car is a marvel – but the original Tuscan could bite in the handling department. The Tuscan 2 features a revised geometry, improved bump stops plus re-rated springs and dampers so that the car can be manhandled more easily when pushing the Tuscan 2 to its limits. But still, it's advised that the TVR is handled with care.

Practical As Well As Powerful

Many supercars require you to shoe-horn any luggage into them using either bespoke bags... or a crowbar. The Tuscan 2 however can happily take two golf bags, which means the car's actually practical as well as sensational.

Lighten Up

The key to the Tuscan 2's searing performance is the fact that it weighs so little – with a kerb weight of only 1,100kg/2425lbs to cart around, that 4-litre straight-six engine can offer supercar performance without the need for added extras.

TVR Tuscan 2: The Specifications

ENGINE	All-aluminium TVR Speed Six straight-six	**BRAKES FRONT**	Ventilated discs with 4-piston alloy callipers/ 304mm/12in	**SUSPENSION REAR**	Independent double wish bones with coils over gas hydraulic dampers & anti-roll bar
DISPLACEMENT	3605cc	**BRAKES REAR**	Ventilated discs with single sliding piston calipers/282mm/11in		
MAXIMUM POWER	350bhp at 7,200rpm			**KERB WEIGHT**	1100kg/2425lbs
MAXIMUM TORQUE	290lb ft at 5,500rpm			**LENGTH**	4235mm/167in
TRANSMISSION	Five-speed manual	**SUSPENSION FRONT**	Independent double wish bones with coils over gas hydraulic dampers & anti-roll bar	**WIDTH**	1810mm/71in
0–60MPH	4.2secs			**HEIGHT**	1200mm/47in
0–100MPH	9.5secs			**WHEELS FRONT**	8 x 16in
MAXIMUM SPEED	175mph			**WHEEL REAR**	8 x 16in
STEERING	Rack and pinion with power assist				

Future Perfect?

It seems like we've hit perfection with the supercar. So where do you go from here? How do you top what seems insurmountable? Well, judging from the various developments and news (and a fair smattering of rumours too), the best is inevitability still to come. The supercar community's desire to outdo each other and seduce buyers will see the arrival of more potential supercar classics over the next few years.

For example, McLaren is all set to re-enter the scene aproper in 2008 with its supercar codenamed the P8. Featuring a Mercedes-sourced 6.3-litre V8, the P8 should be able to produce above 500bhp and over 440lb ft of torque, all for the estimated price of £150,000/US$200,000.

Then there are the left-of-the-middle entries such as Project 1221's MF1. Details are scant about this emerging supercar but the makers claim it will have unmatched handling and agility plus a large luggage capacity. Yes, you may have heard such hyperbole a dozen times before but the MF1 could actually deliver. After all, it's being engineered by the former technical director of Lamborghini and Bugatti, Mauro Forghieri.

As for the far future, there's that 300mph barrier to break, and it has been predicted that supercars will produce in excess of 2,000bhp, weigh 25 percent less than current crop and could even hit 350mph. Sounds like the ramblings of the mad but there is a supercar that's set to touch down later this year which could potentially leave the outrageous performance of current supercars for dead, and offer an enticing and very real glimpse of what the future of the supercar has in store for us...

Enter the Bugatti Veyron.

Bugatti Veyron

Fact or fiction? The latest legend to bear the Bugatti name could finally be with us after a very long development period...

Copyright Bugatti Automobiles S.A.S.

Death in the Bugatti family; a failed revival; and a rebirth followed by a humiliating bankruptcy when the world sank into recession in the 1990s – reading Bugatti's history, you could be forgiven for thinking that the company is cursed. Even in the hands of Volkswagen, the development of the latest car to bear the Bugatti name – the Veyron – was at one point halted. But now VW has the car back on track with delivery of the first Veyron to one lucky (and rich) customer at the end of 2005.

Any supercar fan knows why it's essential that the Veyron does finally touch down – after all, it could potentially rip asunder every supercar that's gone before it. Here are the figures – it's got nearly 1,000bhp on tap; it's got not one, but 4 turbos; it's expected to weigh in at just under 2 tonnes; it can go from 0–60 in an estimated 3secs; it has a potentially record-breaking top speed of over 250mph; it features the biggest rear tyres ever fitted on a production car; it has four wheel drive of course; oh, and it's going to cost in excess of 1,000,000 Euros/US\$1,000,000 to get your hands on one. In fact, everything about this supercar is big – the DSG gearbox even has 7 gears to make the most of (and more importantly, tame) the Veyron's amazing W16, 64v quad-turbo 8-litre engine.

Copyright Bugatti Automobiles S.A.S.

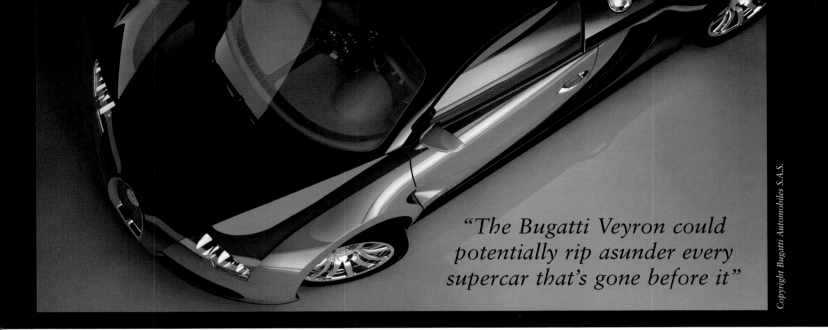

"The Bugatti Veyron could potentially rip asunder every supercar that's gone before it"

Tall Order?

Volkswagen intends to make between 30 to 50 Veyrons a year depending on the demand from customers. And if you're wondering if Volkswagen is actually up to the job of selling supercars, bear in mind that they own Audi – the company that oversaw the creation of the next generation of Lamborghinis.

Back To Its Roots

The Veyron is being assembled at a workshop right next to Chateau St Jean near Molsheim in France – which is the region where the company's founder, Ettore Bugatti, began making his dream cars nearly 100 years ago.

Brake Neck Speeds

With nearly 1,000bhp to propel the driver towards the horizon, it's fairly important that the Veyron can stop as quickly as it can start. To aid in avoiding near disaster when a car pulls out in front of you while you're doing 200mph + on a German autobahn, the Veyron is fitted with specialist carbon-ceramic brakes and a rear wing that can be deployed as an air brake. It is claimed that slamming on the anchors at 248mph will bring the Veyron to a complete standstill in less than 10secs.

Bugatti Veyron (specifications subject to change)

ENGINE	64v quad turbo W16	TRANSMISSION	Seven-speed DSG	HEIGHT	1206mm/47in
VALVETRAIN	DOHC 4 Valves / Cyl	0–60MPH	3.0secs	WHEELS FRONT	9.5 x 20in
DISPLACEMENT	7993cc	MAXIMUM SPEED	252mph	WHEEL REAR	13 x 21in
MAXIMUM POWER	987bhp at 6,000rpm	KERB WEIGHT	1950kg/4299lbs approx.		
MAXIMUM TORQUE	922lb ft at 2,200-5,500rpm	LENGTH	4380mm/172in		
		WIDTH	1994mm/78in		

Supercars on a Budget

Save winning the lottery, it's inevitable that the intoxicating delights of owning a Lamborghini or a Pagani are well out of the reach of most us; for now, at least. But there's no reason to despair (or seriously consider a career in armed robbery) because there are cars out there that can offer similar thrills to the supercar, but for a fraction of the price.

We're featuring four candidates for your deliberation here that cover a lot of the 'supercar bases' such as great (or outlandish) looks, thrilling performances and handling that delights at every corner. And if none of these suit your budget, take solace in the fact that a quick flick through those local classifieds for secondhand cars will reveal some real driving gems. Think Mazda RX-7 or Subaru Impreza Turbo to name but two of the classics available that guarantee maximum fun for minimal money. After all, there's something for everybody to live out those driving dreams. We'll see you on the road…

Ariel Atom 2

No, it's not your typical looking supercar but hey, the British aren't known for settling for the same old, same old...

Perhaps the Atom is the antithesis to the supercar scene's sometimes po-facedness. With no swish bodywork covering up its ultra-lightweight chassis, everything is out on display. Perhaps this is a road-going car that can truly be said to be a perfect example of form following function. And the great thing about the Atom is that its function is so simple – to make you remember why you fell in love with driving in the first place.

The car's unique composite twin seat unit means that you won't find yourself (or your passenger) being thrown all over the cockpit. Well, it's hardly even a cockpit – there are no frills here, merely the basics required to get started.

As for the Atom's performance on the straight stuff, you can see why the car has gone down a storm – the Ariel Atom 2 released in 2003 offers up the perfect performance to help induce

that feel-good factor – after all, it features one of world's finest budget engines (and six-speed gearboxes) whipped straight out of a Japanese-spec Honda Civic Type R, which produces 220bhp. But bear in mind that the Atom weighs only 456kg/1005lbs – with such a lean kerb weight, it makes the likes of Zonda and Enzo look in need of a two-week stint on a 'fat farm'. And just to rub the salt into those supercar wounds, Ariel offers the Atom in an 'enhanced' supercharged version boasting an insane 300bhp. Helmet recommended.

145

"The Ariel Atom 2 features one of the world's finest budget engines whipped straight out of a Japanese-spec Honda Civic Type R"

Ariel Atom 2: The Specifications

ENGINE	Honda iVTEC / 4 Cyl	**MAXIMUM TORQUE**	145lb ft at 6,100rpm	**MAXIMUM SPEED**	135mph
DISPLACEMENT	1998cc	**TRANSMISSION**	Six-speed manual	**KERB WEIGHT**	456kg
MAXIMUM POWER	220bhp at 8,200rpm	**0–60MPH**	3.5secs		

Lotus Exige

Offering outstanding performance on the track, and the ability to be an everyday runabout, the Exige is also packed with racing pedigree...

The miracle makers based in Norfolk, UK, first launched the Lotus Exige in 2000; the mid-engine coupé was actually based on the Mk I Lotus Elise, the firm's critically acclaimed two-seater roadster. In 2004 though, the Exige was relaunched this time featuring a Toyota 1.8-litre VVT-i engine instead of the original's Rover K-series. The bullet-proof Toyota engine generates 189bhp which makes the Exige zip from 0–60 in 4.9secs. The Exige's underpinnings are now based on the Elise Mk II – in fact, the extruded and bonded aluminium tub, with a steel rear subframe, is used in the Elise 111R.

The specially commissioned Lotus Exige Sport features carbon fibre bodywork and front splitter, a rear diffuser, and an adjustable rear wing for added downforce. Instead of the Toyota engine, there's a 400bhp 3-litre V6 lump paired with a sequential six-speed gearbox.

Customers wanting a more extreme version of the standard Exige will have to make do with Exige Sport 240R which features 240hp and a supercar-crushing 0–60 in 3.9secs – do bear in mind though that only 50 will ever see the light of day. So best to get that order in now.

"No corner is too sharp or scary for the Exige. The question isn't whether the car can take it; the real question is can you?"

Lotus Exige:
The Specifications

ENGINE	Aluminium Inline-4
DISPLACEMENT	1796cc
MAXIMUM POWER	189bhp at 7,800rpm
MAXIMUM TORQUE	133.5lb ft at 6,800rpm
TRANSMISSION	Six-speed manual
0-60 MPH	4.9secs
0-100 MPH	13.2secs
MAXIMUM SPEED	147mph
KERB WEIGHT	875kg/1929lbs

Mercedes-Benz SLK350

'Luxury and performance' all wrapped up in mini-supercar looks. The SLK350 is one very special car...

The original SLK was a great car – for posers. Its main party trick was the ability to turn from a coupé into an open-top roadster in seconds thanks to its smart metal retractable roof. The trouble was, for all its sporty pretensions, it could never match the might of the sublime Porsche Boxster. Enter the SLK MkII.

It's those looks – the original SLK may have been a smart if slightly effeminate design, but the SLK MkII is far more like a muscular roadster thanks to its F1-style nose 'inspired' by its (very) big brother, the SLR. The folding metal roof remains and is now more of an elegant design – and more importantly, it goes up quickly in case rain interrupts play.

The entry model SLK200 powered by a supercharged 1.8-litre is best suited to those who want more show than go. It provides adequate performance for a droptop – 0-60 in 8.3secs – but hardly the kind of acceleration that will trouble a sporty family sedan, never mind a full-blooded supercar with a V12. No, the model to aim for is the rather fine SLK350. Featuring a warbling 3.5-litre V6, the torque-happy engine offers plenty of power for the thrill seeker.

The SLK also now has a quality six-speed gearbox as standard for the driver who likes to feel absolutely in control of that V6 in front of him. Mercedes claims that the auto shaves 0.1secs off the 0-60 time. Whether it shaves some of the fun off too is open to debate.

"The SLK350 is a near-perfect blend; a bruiser when you're in the mood and an extremely comfortable cruiser when you're not"

Mercedes-Benz SLK350: The Specifications

ENGINE	V6
DISPLACEMENT	3498cc
MAXIMUM POWER	272bhp at 6,000rpm
MAXIMUM TORQUE	258lb ft at 2,400rpm
TRANSMISSION	Six-speed manual/
	Seven-speed auto
0-60 MPH	5.6secs
MAXIMUM SPEED	155mph
KERB WEIGHT	1465kg/3231lbs

Vauxhall VX220 Turbo

Supercar performance, but at a fraction of the price. Discover the small car guaranteed to deliver big grins...

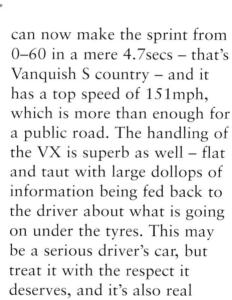

Welcome to the rather brilliant Vauxhall VX220 Turbo. It's all the more remarkable if you consider the car's manufacturer – Vauxhall (owned by General Motors), in the UK, has been perceived for decades as a rather run-of-the-mill car manufacturer.

So creating excitement became the job of the original VX220 launched in 2000. On the face of it, Vauxhall should have struggled to produce such a fantastic two-seater roadster but they had help – they went to Lotus.

Featuring an aluminium chassis and plastic body panels, the original VX220 had a 2.2-litre engine that could do 0-60 in 5.6secs. But that wasn't powerful enough for Vauxhall... so they released the VX220 Turbo. Featuring 197bhp from the 2-litre turbo engine, the car can now make the sprint from 0–60 in a mere 4.7secs – that's Vanquish S country – and it has a top speed of 151mph, which is more than enough for a public road. The handling of the VX is superb as well – flat and taut with large dollops of information being fed back to the driver about what is going on under the tyres. This may be a serious driver's car, but treat it with the respect it deserves, and it's also real controllable fun.

In 2004, Vauxhall released an even hotter version of the VX, the VXR220, which could hit 0-60 in only 4.2secs and only ran out of puff at 154mph. Alas, due to its limited production number of 65 cars, they all sold out in six weeks – typical supercar then.

"Vauxhall should have struggled to produce such a fantastic two-seater roadster but they had help... they went to Lotus"

Vauxhall VX220 Turbo: The Specifications

ENGINE	Inline-4
DISPLACEMENT	1998cc
MAXIMUM POWER	197bhp at 5,500rpm
MAXIMUM TORQUE	184lb ft from 1,950rpm
TRANSMISSION	Six-speed manual
0-60 MPH	4.7secs
0-100 MPH	Under 13secs
MAXIMUM SPEED	151mph
KERB WEIGHT	930kg/2050lbs